THE RESURRECTION
AND
MODERN MAN

**IGNATIUS IV
PATRIARCH OF ANTIOCH**

THE RESURRECTION AND MODERN MAN

translated
by
STEPHEN BIGHAM

with a foreword
by
OLIVIER CLEMENT

ST VLADIMIR'S SEMINARY PRESS
CRESTWOOD, NEW YORK 10707
1985

Published under the title
La Résurrection et l'homme d'aujourd'hui
Desclée de Brouwer 1981

Library of Congress Cataloging in Publication Data

Ignatius IV, Patriarch of Antioch, 1921-
The Resurrection and modern man.

Translation of: La résurrection et l'homme
d'aujourd'hui.

1. Church renewal—Orthodox Church—Addresses, essays,
lectures. 2. Jesus Christ—Resurrection—Addresses, essays,
lectures. 3. Orthodox Eastern Church—Doctrines—Addresses,
essays, lectures. 4. Antioch (Orthodox patriarchate)—
Doctrines—Addresses, essays, lectures.
I. Title.
BX323.13613 1985   269   85-8387
ISBN 0-88141-048-9

THE RESURRECTION AND MODERN MAN

© Copyright 1985

by

ST VLADIMIR'S SEMINARY PRESS

ISBN 0-88141-048-9

PRINTED IN THE UNITED STATES OF AMERICA
BY
ATHENS PRINTING COMPANY
NEW YORK, NY

Contents

Foreword

I would especially like to thank the patriarchate of Antioch for allowing us to publish these two fundamental essays: "Behold, I Make All Things New" and "The Resurrection: Its Meaning for Modern Man." These texts remind the West of the basic kerygma of our faith; and they do so in the language of its own problems, but with an intense yet simple lyricism that stresses the victory of Christ over hell and death—all forms of death; and the Church as sacrament of the resurrection, where the realm of death is transformed into the realm of Breath, which here and now can make us living beings . . .

Today this message has all the more weight because on July 2, 1979, under the name of Ignatius IV, its author became the Orthodox Patriarch of Antioch, the third ranking hierarch of the Orthodox Church after the patriarchs of Constantinople and Alexandria.

It was at Antioch, whose Church with its Petrine and Pauline foundation preceded that of Rome, that the two pre-eminent apostles, Peter and Paul, confronted each other in a dispute that was decided by the council of the Apostles in Jerusalem. It was at Antioch that the disciples of Jesus were first called Christians (Acts 11:26). At the beginning of the 2nd century, thanks to the letters of the first Ignatius, St Ignatius the God-bearer, we perceive at Antioch the integration of the people of God into the body of Christ. This body is spoken of as a eucharistic community presided over by the ministry of the bishop, who is both the image of Christ and the image of the Father. At the same time, we perceive how St Ignatius defined the priority of Rome as a "presidency of love," as the see that watches over the communion of all the local Churches. Antioch became the center of an immense missionary expansion in all the East, as well as in Syria, Mesopotamia, Armenia, and the Caucasus. At the first Ecumenical Council in 325 A.D., Antioch was recognized as the primal see in a region with a predominantly semitic civilization. Rome was to play the same role in the Latin world; Alexandria enjoyed primacy in Egypt; and Constantinople, some time later, was to exercise this role in the Greek-speaking world, even though the Greek language was the bearer of culture throughout the eastern Mediterranean area.

In the whole of the Christian world and then in the whole Orthodox world, Antioch gave witness to a concrete biblical and semitic vision of Christianity, demonstrating how superficial it is to define the Orthodox world as simply "greco-slavic." During the great patristic age, what is rather improperly called the "school of Antioch" refused the allegorizing method of interpretation in order to remain close to the biblical sense of mystery within history. Antiochian theology, then and today, holds to an exegesis that is not strictly literal but rather typological and pneumatological. Thereby it remains profoundly attached to the humanity of Christ and to the christology of man. St John

Chrysostom, first a deacon and then a priest in Antioch before becoming archbishop of Constantinople, refused to separate the "sacrament of the altar" from the "sacrament of the brother." He takes quite literally Matt 25, where the poor man appears as "another Christ." Significantly, St John's sacramental realism leads him likewise to call the priest at the altar "another Christ." It is in an Antiochian environment that the properly biblical idea of "the heart" won out over the notion of "the intellect" to designate the center of human existence, where one both opens oneself and is gathered into personal unity. It was the Syrians, hellenized in language but not in their inner sensibility, who from the 6th to the 8th centuries created a rich yet refined hymnography that became integrated into the Byzantine liturgy. Therefore in the 12th century, when this Byzantine liturgy was adopted by the Orthodox patriarchate of Antioch, it represented something of a return on an investment. In fact, the eucharistic liturgy which is most widely used in the Orthodox Church is the one assembled and written by St John Chrysostom.

In the 5th and 6th centuries, parallel hierarchies were set up for the first time on Antiochian territory. This was the result of the "monophysite" schism which, as we see today, rested on a doctrinal misunderstanding. It served, however, as a justification for a separate Syriac identity set over against the Greek empire. This confrontation was actually the result of the friction caused by the meeting of two different cultures and two systems of thinking. For those who remained faithful to pan-Orthodoxy as it had been expressed at the Council of Chalcedon, Christ was thought of as one single person in two natures, human and

divine; while for the "monophysites," he was conceived
as one single divine-human reality (physis). This
separate Syriac identity was still very much alive in the
8th century when another faction of Syriac Christianity,
faithful in nearly every aspect to Chalcedon, acquired
its autonomy and became the Maronite Church. This
Church was later to become attached to Rome during
the Crusades. From that time on, the Orthodox patriarchate of Antioch has been designated as "Greek"
and "melkite." "Melkite" comes from a semitic root
meaning "king" or "emperor," and refers to the fact
that the patriarchate belonged to the Church of the
Byzantine empire, at least until the Moslem conquest.
The word "Greek" even today refers to the fact that
this patriarchate is part of the whole Orthodox Church
in which the patriarch of Constantinople has a primacy
of honor. The local liturgical language, however, after
having been Syriac for many centuries, finally became
Arabic in the 16th century. The patriarchate of Antioch
is now, and desires only to be, *Arabic Orthodoxy*.

Since the Moslem conquest in the 7th century, this
Arabic Church has been freed from any political-reli-
gious triumphalism and has been living under the
dhimma i.e. a condition of autonomy, granted to the
"people of the book," but under the supervision of
Islam. This status in no way hampered the patriarchate
from creating with the help of St John of Damascus, a
synthesis of Greek patristics. The "summa" of St John
was to serve as the basic theological text for the Orthodox Church throughout its whole medieval period.
Thanks to this synthesis, the Church of Antioch was
also able to safeguard, in opposition to Byzantine icon-
oclasm, the meaning of the icon. This achievement

was an admirable sign of solidarity with the whole of Orthodoxy especially from a Church whose spiritual semitism was and remains more sensitive to the Word than to the Image.

Following the tormenting period of the Crusades, with the forced Latinization which the crusaders brought with them, and following the Mongol invasion that destroyed the city of Antioch, the seat of the patriarchate was transferred to Damascus in 1322. It is still there today, located in a high but hidden enclosure which symbolizes the effacement of the *dhimma*.

In the 18th century, this weakened Church had to withstand the assault of uniatism. Since the end of the Middle Ages, Rome has ceased to look for dialogue on a Church to Church basis and has no longer accepted the idea of a council of unity that assumed the existence of a real if compromised existence of one single Church. Taking the advantage of its cultural superiority, Rome sought to bring into existence small groups of Eastern Christians under its jurisdiction. In 1724, as a result of this policy, a Greek Melkite Catholic Church was created. In the 19th century, the ultimate wound was to be inflicted on the patriarchate of Antioch in the form of proselytism, hostile to the values of the East, that was unleashed by Catholic, Anglican, and Protestant missionaries. Taking into account the tragic migration of the Armenian Church, these Western missionary activities brought to fourteen the number of Christian groups co-existing and mixing together on the territory of Antioch. Such a plurality of voices could, of course, only obscure the face of Christ in the eyes of the Moslems. In this whole affair, the strength of the Orthodox patriarchate was to affirm its Arabic character: in the 19th century, Antioch was in a more advantageous position than its neighbor in Jerusalem because it was able to obtain Arabic bishops. It was to the Arabs and especially to the Orthodox Christians, that the task fell of assuring the cultural and national renaissance—*Nahda*—that restored the Arabic character of the area; a task accomplished in resistence to the occupying Turks. As a result of this renaissance, Arabic has become a modern language.

Shortly before the Second World War, during the period of the French mandate in Syria and Lebanon, the Greek Orthodox Church seemed to be stultified and exhausted, just a small piece in the sociological puzzle that made up the political and religious mosaic of the Middle East. Intelligence and modernity seemed to be on the side of Catholicism. Moreover, it was in the Catholic schools, where teaching was in French that the children of well-to-do Orthodox families were educated. Then, almost miraculously, the renaissance began. Some closely associated students, clerics and laymen, almost completely disheartened by the inertia of their Church, discovered the latent power of Orthodoxy through reading French language theological works by the great theologians and religious philosophers of the Russian emigration, especially the book *The Orthodox Church* by Fr Sergius Bulgakov. In July, 1942, they decided to found the Movement of Orthodox Youth of the Patriarchate of Antioch. This prophetic and charismatic movement, one of whose founders is the present patriarch of Antioch, was by no means a marginal group, for right from the beginning it worked at the very heart of the Church. Its first achievement was to rediscover the personal and communal meaning of the eucharist through a practice of frequent communion which then was extremely rare. The activity of the group involved not only catechetical instruction and pastoral work; it also dealt with a deepening spiritual awareness and theological reflection that was at one and the same time traditional and concerned with problems of the contemporary world. The method of the Movement was very much in keeping with the Antiochian character. The members were thoroughly conscious of their Christian Arab orientation and their place within universal Orthodoxy. Their approach took many forms: sending students to St Sergius' Institute in Paris; committing themselves to and frequently assuming leadership positions in Syndesmos, the world federation of Orthodox youth movements; frequently visiting in and sending to Lebanon spiritual leaders and theologians from southeast and western Europe, such as Fr Andrew Scrima and especially Fr Lev Gillet, known as "a monk of the Eastern Church," etc. Young people from Beirut regularly went into the mountain villages where there were no longer any priests, in order to revive the churches, pray with the people and to instruct the young. Very soon, priests began to emerge from their ranks; then monks began to appear where monastic life had long before seemed dead. In 1952, the foundation of the convent of Mar Yacub near Tripoli was laid, and then in 1959, a monastery at Deir al Harf near Beirut was started. In 1970, a theological institute was opened in Balamand under the patronage of St John of Damascus. Soon bishops were installed, and finally in 1979 Ignatius IV became patriarch.

Ignatius IV (Hazim) was born in 1921 in the village of Mhardey near Hama in Syria. He comes from one of those families that had faithfully preserved the Orthodox faith and offered an example of high moral conduct based on a serious and deep Christian ethic. Very soon, the young Ignatius was attracted to service within the Church. While studying in Beirut towards a degree in literature, he entered the service of the local diocese, becoming an acolyte and then a deacon. From 1942 on, he was one of the leading figures of the Movement of Orthodox Youth. In 1945, he was sent to Paris where he studied at St Sergius Institute. There he discovered both the neopatristic synthesis and an ecclesiology of communion, theological perspectives that have now become widespread throughout the patriarchate of Antioch. He also came into contact with Orthodox thought that was both open and creative. He has since been able to appropriate that thought and bring it to fruition in an original way in his personal writings as we can readily see in the following pages. From his time at St Sergius, Ignatius was moved by a desire not only to transmit the deposit of faith, but also to take Orthodoxy out of its unhistorical ghetto by discovering in the spirit of Holy Tradition living answers to the challenges of modern life, a modern life that has left its tragic mark on the Middle East in the form of practical secularization, the Palestinian drama, the rise of Marxism, and finally a renewed Islamic ideology.

Upon his return to Lebanon, Ignatius Hazim became the founder and first rector of the Balmand seminary. There he strove to provide the patriarchate with responsible leaders who had received good spiritual and intellectual training and who were witnesses to an awakened and deeply personal faith. He became a bishop in 1961 and metropolitan of Lattaquiey, in Syria, in 1970. Both Moslems and Christians welcomed him with great joy. The new metropolitan was a reserved but friendly man, who manifested a deep and courageous straightforwardness; he was simple, direct, and down-to-earth. His style broke with the former tradition of episcopal grandeur, and he inaugurated an authentic practice of frequent communion. After his election to the patriarchate, he is quoted as saying:

> I know that I will be judged if I do not carry the Church and each one of you in my heart. It is not possible for me to address you as if I were different from you. No difference separates us. I am an integral part of you; I am in you; and I ask you to be in me. For the Lord comes, and the Spirit descends on the brothers gathered, united in communion, as they manifest a diversity of charisms in the unity of the Spirit.

When the historical tragedy of war came to Lebanon, Ignatius, the local bishop and then patriarch, adopted an especially firm attitude, witnessing to non-violence and to evangelical love at the heart of Arabic tradition. With the Moslems, he hoped to develop new relations founded on the spiritual concept of man (as the "image of God" for the Christians and "vicar of God" for the Moslems). The goal of this effort was to work in common for the establishment of a more open and more just society, for the deepening of Arab culture capable of drawing deeply from its own sources and thus developing the capacity of mastering the material world.

At the same time, Ignatius IV worked to renew his Church that numbered six dioceses in Lebanon, six in Syria, four in North and South America, and four patriarchal delegations in Western Europe, Mexico, Brazil, and Australia, totaling some 1,500,000 faithful. The patriarch has given a new dynamism to the Holy Synod and hopes that it will name bishops who are close to the people and are motivated to develop the Church's ecclesial and spiritual life, detached from political factions. He seeks pastors and not a cultural elite. This has already been achieved in Beirut, with the election of the young metropolitan Elias Audi, a man of vigor who is close to the people. The Church is thus slowly disengaging itself from the crushing sociological milieu that had become normative in the Middle East, and it is dedicating itself to its spiritual mission, a mission which must transform the attitude of the people towards political, social, and cultural life. Such a mission should enable the Church gradually to assume the role of peace-maker within society.

But this cannot be done alone. The renewed Greek patriarchate of Antioch, while stressing the need for Orthodox solidarity in the Middle East and throughout the world, does not intend to close its borders as a community. Patriarch Ignatius IV, co-president of the Council of Middle Eastern Churches and a member of the Central Committee of the World Council of Churches, is a man of dialogue. The ardent meditation that unfolds in the following pages on the words of Revelation, "Behold, I make all things new," is an appeal addressed to all Christians. One of the major preoccupations of Ignatius IV is to re-establish Antiochian unity by means of a genuine rapproachment with the pre-

Chalcedonians, as well as with the Churches united to Rome, whose attitude has changed considerably since Vatican II. More and more, these Churches are affirming their Eastern roots; and they are finding in their ranks persons who are fully dedicated to Antiochian unity, such as Fr John Corbon, whose recent book on the liturgy, *Liturgie de Source*, is properly speaking, a book of the undivided Church. It is no longer a question of ecumenism in the general sense of the word; rather, as the future patriarch affirmed in Vienna, in a statement made in October 1978, to the institute "Pro Oriente," we are actually in a "preconciliar" age, one that must result in a "plurality in unity," to recall the title of another work of Fr Corbon. This will mean a plural unity as well for the Church of the Arabs. In the mind of Ignatius IV, the Antiochian communities must achieve a "communion of love" that will permit the basic kerygma to be distinguished from later approaches. This basic kerygma is that of the great Councils of the undivided Church, which include Chalcedon. Once elucidated, such a kerygma will finally be "received" by all. The later approaches also, when rectified or understood according to their own patterns of thought can be similarly admitted in their legitimate diversity. According to the thought of the patriarch, this will only be possible by means of a thoroughgoing renewal of pneumatology and pentecostal dynamism that will conquer the fear and suspicion that the notion "pentecostal" provokes. We should not forget that at Antioch Peter and Paul opposed each other and were reconciled. Nor should we overlook the fact that it was Antioch which from the beginning knew how to properly define the role of Rome; or that it was the patriarch of

Antioch who, in 1054, was convinced that the problem of the filioque, far from breaking off eucharistic communion, could only find its true solution through continued communion. This Antioch may well become the laboratory for the reconstitution of original Christian unity. Even now we can affirm that Ignatius IV stands as a powerful witness to this Antiochian spirituality, whose main elements can be summed up: 1.) as a great sensitivity to mystery, but a mystery filled with light, like the brilliant white light reflected from the churches and mosques of Damascus, an all-consuming light that is nothing less than a theophany of the Holy Trinity; 2.) as an equally deep sense of "kenosis" or self-effacement, accepted as an act of total love by our Lord, felt and expressed by His people with all the semitic realism of the flesh and of history; it is equally a self-affacement of the Spirit within the tragic history of the Church, an effacement brought about by the *dhimma* and of Beirut torn apart by so many battles; 3.) as a sensitivity to the mystery of violent askesis and chastity, that stands apart from a sensual and corrupt society to embrace values shown forth in the life of the Virgin Mary and in monasticism (Islam has also proven sensitive to such ascetic values); and finally 4.) as sensitivity to the appeal of the Old Testament prophets for justice; a sensitivity that stresses the word over the icon, or rather the certitude that each human person who answers the call of God, constitutes a veritable icon.

We can also feel the corresponding vocation of Antioch: its witness in the heart of Islam, a witness of patient *dhimmi* who have come out of their isolation. Are they not called today to reveal to the Moslems that Christ has come for everyone, that He is the revelation of divine compassion, who transcends his own transcendance in order to liberate us from death through His own death upon the Cross?

Antioch now has an Orthodox patriarch worthy of its history and of its vocation. It is in the light of this great history and the high hopes which Ignatius IV evokes that we should read the following pages.

OLIVIER CLEMENT

PART ONE

"Behold, I Make All Things New"

Introduction *

At the opening of the 4th Assembly and in solidarity with the world, let us look at things from the perspective of the visionary of Patmos, from St John's point of view in the midst of the great tribulation of the first century; let us also listen to Him who sits on the throne and declares: "Behold, I make all things new." (Rev 21:5)

We cannot understand this affirmation as a mere program for study and action: such an interpretation would lead us to the dead end of established orders and revolutions, that is, to simple moralizing. No; the affirmation, "I make all things new," is not a program; it is an event, in fact the only Event of history. The heavens and the earth pass away; everything wears out and passes away; but the Word of the living God, the New Creation, does not pass away.

We propose to be neither archeologists of Christianity nor sociologists of a revolutionary Church: all that is radically outdated. We must instead be prophets of the New Creation and visionaries of the resurrected Christ.

What is this Event of the New Creation, and how does it call us to renewal today?

*The Opening Address of the 4th Assembly of the World Council of Churches, Uppsala, Sweden; July, 1968.

CHAPTER 1

The New Creation

The New Creation comes not from the world of cause and effect nor from the will of man, but from God and from Him alone. It is remarkable that this statement "Behold, I make all things new," is the only one in Revelation which is made by Him "who sits on the throne." All other revelations of this book are given to John by an angel, "a fellow servant like yourself" (Rev 22:8-9); or else they are proclaimed by Lord Jesus (Rev 1:11 and 22:16). If we search the New Testament for the "moments" in which the Father Himself speaks, we find only three:

1. The "moment" of Jesus' baptism: "Behold, a voice from heaven said, 'This is my beloved Son with whom I am well pleased'" (Mt 3:17, Mk 1:11, and Lk 3:22).

2. The "moment" of the Transfiguration: "This is my beloved Son in whom I am well-pleased; listen to Him" (Mt 17:5, Mk 9:7, Lk 9:35; cf. 2 Pt 1:17-18).

3. The "moment," rather the supreme "hour" of Holy Pascha, when all things are

recreated by the Event of the New Creation:
"Then a voice came from heaven saying, 'I have
glorified Him, and I will glorify Him again'"
(Jn 12:28-30); Jesus then adds, "It is not for
me that this voice was heard but for you" (Jn
12:30).

It was indeed for us that Jesus "sent his Angel to
proclaim . . . these revelations concerning the Churches"
(Rev 22:16), along with the revelation that gives birth
to all other revelations: "Behold, I make all things
new!" This word must be much more than just a theme
for study and prayer. It must give us life, movement,
and being. It is God's creative Word itself, not only
for tomorrow, for the end time; it exercises its creative
power today and has been active "from the beginning."

This creative Word of the Father, revealed in the
beloved Son when the fullness of time had come, "is
always at work" (Jn. 5:17). It was at work in the time
of the Old Testament prefigurations, when it was known
in the "shadows" (Col 2:17) and in the cloud; just
as it is at work now, in the "last time," made known in
the transfiguring epiphany of Him who has come. The
Revelations of St John unveil the meaning of history.
The Lamb is the only one who can receive the book of
history from the hand of Him who sits on the throne,
and can open the seals (Rev 5:7-9). The ultimate
revelation of the creative Word enlightens all preceding
history and gives it meaning. Peter, himself one of the
witnesses of the Transfiguration, contemplated Christ
as "the lamb without spot, perceived from the foundation of the world, and manifested in the last times" for
our sake (1 Pt 1:19-20).

To help us recall, if need be, that this New Creation "sustains the universe" (Heb 1:3) and "recapitulates all things" (Eph 1:10), we should focus our attention on three biblical texts that can be interpreted in the light of Rev 21:5.

1. *Genesis 1:1*. "In the beginning, God created the heavens and the earth." Here we have the same divine action (epoiesen) and the same all-encompassing reality of "the heavens and the earth" that we find in the reference of Rev 21:5 to "all things." In both passages appears the same revelation of newness: "In the beginning"; and "behold" (idou), which is a biblical term frequently used to express the advent from God of a new creative act. In its first words about the creation, the Torah contains the complete mystery that was to be revealed in subsequent history; the Torah is not just a journal of religious archeology, but the normative revelation of the meaning of all events. Today, as for the priestly author of Genesis 1, the living God creates all things "in the beginning." He is utterly different from any "first cause" that sets into motion a series of derivative causes: this vision of the created order is archaic and meaningless. For God is rather the creative newness within all that exists. He sustains all things by his powerful Word: "He is before all things, and all things subsist in Him" (Col 1:17).

The New Creation, then, is not what we create when we take an already existing reality and transform it into something new; nor is it the result of refashioning an outmoded reality to bring it up to date. The New Creation consists rather in the fact that the Lord acts and speaks within all reality, whether things or persons. He does so as the source of the "river of life, bright as crystal, flowing from the throne of God and of the Lamb" (Rev 22:1). We shall never attain the New Creation so long as we fail to live and experience what we might call "the dialogical structure of the cosmos." The living God truly speaks and acts. *Dabar Yahweh, Logos tou Kyriou,* this one divine reality is inseparably Word and Event. What exists, *exists for us* because it was *spoken to us* by Him. To live in and experience our world only at the level of phenomena and causes is to remain outside and beyond this relationship of "dialogue," between the Logos and ourselves. It is in fact to remain in death, the only truly "old" and "worn out" reality the Bible knows.

2. *Isaiah 43:19.* In contrast, the new revelation is presented to us in this text of deutero-Isaiah. This passage was written during the exile, that terrible experience of death which contradicted all the promises of life given by the Word of God.

We ourselves are still in this exile. If our vision remains fixed on ground level, at the level of mere phenomena, we will not even catch the tragic irony inherent in the world of objects. From the moment that everything becomes "objective," it can only mean the exile and alienation of the person. Whether we be consumers or revolutionaries, technocrats or members of underdeveloped nations, we are tempted to reduce everything to an object, including our own inner life. We investigate objects, and discover the absurd. Then all things become thoroughly dead: the world, man, even God. Everything becomes old, insofar as it is cut off from its roots in the New and personal Creation. "They have forgotten me, the very source of living waters . . ." (Jer 2:13).

It was within this very period of exile in Babylon that God announced His New Creation. "Remember not the former things, nor consider the things of old. Behold, I am doing something new; now it springs forth, do you not perceive it?" (Is 43:18-19) In this text, we find the same divine action (poieo) and the same outpouring of newness (idou) that we find in Genesis 1:1 and Rev 21:5. What is unique to this passage of Isaiah is that, at one and the same time, it goes beyond the past and announces the near future. In fact, this promise will be fulfilled by the Jewish return from exile in the middle of the 6th century.

For us, however, this passage retains its prophetic value in the present through its very fulfillment. The "something new" which has finally appeared is Christ, and the true return from exile is His resurrection. This is what has been accomplished for us. What has not been abolished however, is our condition of being in exile. The realization of the promise in the person of the resurrected Christ simply enables us to see more clearly the apocalyptic struggle that we are engaged in. We are still living under the sign of the promise. If the prophecy of Isaiah announced not only the historical return from exile in Babylon, but also the coming of Christ the Servant, then the Spirit of the promise presently dwelling in us announces here and now the second coming of Christ the Savior. The expectation has not been abolished. To the contrary, it is revealed and experienced all the more accutely insofar as Christ is already present among us.

Today the Prince of life confronts the Prince of this world. In Christ, death has been overcome, but among those who are of the lineage of the Woman of the

Apocalypse, it still has to be definitively conquered (Rev 12:17). The structure of this world is thus not just "logical," that is animated by the gift of the Logos, but it is also "demonological," held in the power of the *Diabolos*. If we do not take this fact into account, our response to the Word of God will be nothing more than ecclesiastical triumphalism or pathological repentance. In other words, the New Creation "appears" in history as a battle against death; thus it can only be properly conceived as a paschal drama.

3. *2 Cor 5:17.* We now come to the third passage which forms the background to Rev 21:5. "If anyone is in Christ, he is a new creation; the old has passed away, behold, the new has come." Here the verb "to make" is replaced by a noun that implies action: "the creation" (ktisis): the totality of the creation has been personalized ("anyone" and "Christ"). The New Creation is announced by the *idou,* "behold," of Isaiah as well as by contrast with the past (*ta archaia,* the old things); but Paul tells us positively that everything comes from God (5:18). To express this mystery of the New Creation, he uses a term that refers to birth, *gegonen;* the Greek perfect tense denotes an action accomplished in the past but whose effects and results are operative in the present: "a new even has occurred." Certain variant readings of this text such as "everything is new," brings us very close to the literal text of Revelation 21:5.

We should note that in these two passages, 2 Cor 5:17 and Rev 2:15, the promise of Isaiah 43:19 is fulfilled: the past is forgotten, and "the former things have passed away" (Rev 21:4). Yet the main point of 2 Cor 5:17 is to reveal to us the why and the how of this passing, of this transformation: Christ has died to the old world, and His resurrection has inaugurated the New Creation by reconciling everything and everyone to His Father (2 Cor 5:14-21). *The "Passover" of Jesus is the ultimate Event of the New Creation.*

In the light of these passages, is it possible to enter more fully into this Event: "Behold, I make all things new"?

1. First of all, the texts reveal the New Creation within the flow of history. We can sum up as follows the conditions of that Creation that co-exist with us who live in "the last times." The event of the New Creation, the creative energy of the Logos-"Pantocrator" (a term we often find in Revelation), acts "in the beginning" of everything. The structure of the world is "dialogical," in the strictly theological sense of *Logos*. The event of the New Creation penetrates into the darkness; but it is resisted and fought against, because the structure of our world is also diabolical in the strictly theological sense of *Diabolos*.

The event of the New Creation has been accomplished once and for all in the death and resurrection of the Incarnate Logos. Henceforth, therefore, the structure of history is *paschal*, in the strictly theological sense of "passover," a passage from this present world into the New Creation.

Finally, the event of the New Creation, as it is revealed in Rev 21:5, unceasingly and progressively penetrates into this world so that for the person who in faith sees Christ, the consummation of the New Creation is certain; it will be definitive and total. Thus the present structure of history is already "parousial" in the strictly theological sense of *parousia*, that is the presence of God-with-mankind.

2.   Another obvious point that stands out in this biblical vision of history is that the transfiguring power of the New Creation is explained not by the past, but by the future. It is clear that the action of the living God can only be transfiguring and creative. But the marvel of God who revealed himself in Abraham, Isaac and Jacob is that His creative act comes from the future; it is prophetic. God "comes" into the world; He is before us, and we go out to meet Him who calls us, who quickens us, who sends us out, who makes us grow, and who liberates us. Any other god than the Lord is a false god, an idol, a dead god. And it is high time that our modern consciousness bury him. This multiform god, who lives in the "old consciousness of man, in fact stands behind man as a mere cause. This old god dominates, organizes, leads man backwards, and finally alienates him. There is nothing prophetic about this god; on the contrary, he always follows after as the ultimate reason for the unexplainable or as the last recourse for irresponsible people and their actions. This false transcendence is as old as death itself; it is an idol made by the hands of man and for which man feels a passionate jealousy (Gen 3). This false transcendence is a lying work of the devil and not of the truth-bearing Logos. This god is dead, radically dead; yet he will not die historically until all things have been renewed and transfigured. There is no real theology concerning this dead god. Yet the transfiguring power of the New Creation comes into the world, with the world. It does not invent itself nor does it need to prove itself: it simply reveals itself. We welcome it or

we refuse it, but it nevertheless comes as an event. This is why the final word of the Bible can only be an apocalypse, a revelation. "He is and he comes": this is the theme of the final book of the Bible; it is the key to history and the meaning of the truly New Creation.

3. The transfiguring power of the New Creation is the living God, but the arrival of this power in our world is Christ, who is the Father's incarnate and death-conquering Logos. Irenaeus of Lyon says that we are to "know that He has given us something completely new by giving us Himself, He who had been announced in former times: He is the new principle of life which was to come, to renew and enliven humanity" (*Against Heresies,* IV:34, 1). In a similar vein, Maximus the Confessor declared: "In the mystery of the incarnate Word are found the fulfillment of the enigmas and the figures of Scripture as well as the knowledge of sensate and intelligible creatures. He who knows the mystery of the Cross and the tomb knows the *raison d'etre* of these creatures. But he who has been initiated into the hidden power of the resurrection knows the ultimate foundation upon which God, in His plan for creation, establishes all things" (Chapters on the Theology and the Economy of the Son of God Incarnate: 66).

In these last days that we are living through, "the hidden power of the resurrection" is the event of the New Creation. It would be appropriate to reread all the passages in which St Paul speaks of this energy of the resurrection that has been spread throughout the world by the Gospel. This means that in every event of our lives, the Incarnate Word enters into our world of death to participate in death. Jesus really dies; by this in-breaking of the living God, the slavery of man is abolished. The many chains of human captivity—the devil, sin, death, law, and "the flesh" in St Paul's meaning of the word—are broken. The Cross marked the "hour" of the New Creation; the eschaton, the age to come, has entered into our time and has burst asunder our tombs. This death is our resurrection: "Behold, through the cross, joy has come into all the world" (Orthodox paschal service, 6th ode). What is most urgent for us today is to rediscover "the immeasurable greatness of His power in us who believe according to the working of His great might which He accomplished in Christ when He raised Him from the dead" (Eph 1:19-20).

The resurrection is the inauguration of the parousia in our time, and that is why we can both wait with certitude and yet be impatient for its full accomplishment as announced by Him who sits on the throne (Rev 21:5). Because of this certitude, "we await a Savior, the Lord Jesus Christ, who will transform our lowly body to be like His glorious body, by the power which enables Him even to subject all things to Himself" (Phil 3:20-21).

4. How can the paschal event, having accomplished once and for all, become ours today? It happens through the very one who is the fashioner of that event, both at the beginning and in the fulness of time: the Holy Spirit. He is personally the New Creation at work in the world. He is the presence of God-with-us, "joined to our spirit" (Rom 8:16). Without Him, God is far off, Christ is in the past, the gospel is a dead letter, the Church is only an organization, authority is domination, mission is propaganda, worship is a mere mouthing of words, and Christian action is a slave morality.

But with Him, and in indispensable symphony with Him, the cosmos is raised up and groans with the birth pains of the kingdom; man struggles against the "flesh," Christ is raised, the gospel becomes the power of life, the Church offers communion with the Trinity, authority becomes a liberating service, mission becomes a pentecost, the liturgy is lived as both a memorial and an anticipation, and human action is deified.

The Holy Spirit ushers in the parousia by an epiclesis which is both sacramental and mystically concrete. He bestows life, He speaks by the prophets, He situates all things in dialogue with God, He creates communion by offering Himself, and He orients all things towards the Second Coming. "He is the Lord and giver of life" (Nicene Creed). It is by Him that the Church and the world cry out from the depths of their being: "Come, Lord Jesus!" (Rev 22:17-20).

5. The energy of the Holy Spirit introduces a new dimension and a new dynamism into our flat, horizontal world. This divine energy is at once wholly other and yet interior to our world. This point is extremely important not only for a proper understanding of the event we hear about in the Book of Revelation, but also, and especially for, an effective living out of the first signs of this new dynamism in our own times. Revelation with the whole human drama described in its pages, takes place on two levels: that of concrete phenomena and that of divine mystery. On the first level, the world is caused and determined, according to a "structuralist" model. On this level, the chemistry of culture and economics can only transform one form of death into another. But there exists as well the level of mystery on which, ever since Daniel, the visionaries

of the Son of Man discern the creative action of Him who comes and snatches us from the jaws of death.

These two levels are not superimposed on one another; they show rather the principle of the prophetic reading of history, yesterday and today. Let us note that Revelation in its second part (chapters 4-22), is divided into five books, each book having seven parts. We are dealing here with the fifth book, built on seven visions, each one being introduced by the words "Then I saw. . . ." Our text, Rev 21:5, is part of the seventh vision. The literary principle that St John's book is built on is chronological succession. Thus this surprising affirmation, "Behold I make all things new," is not to be relegated into the future beyond history; it reveals the new world which, starting from the present, enters into the sphere of our own temporal order.

The dramatic tension in which we are living therefore, is not situated between a conceptual transcendence and a phenomenal immanence; it is located between two levels of time; 1) this present age (ho aion outos) which is both dialogical and diabolical; and 2) the new time which is "parousial" and which renders this present age "paschal." The agent of this tension, He who has inaugurated it, is the Holy Spirit. This new age, moreover, is more than just a permanent revolution; it is a regeneration, a veritable recreation (Mt 19:28 and Tt 3:5).

Previously, we thought we could safeguard the transcendance of God by identifying Him with "exteriority." Today, in reaction, we would like to preserve "interiority" by identifying Him with immanence. We should refuse this ruinous "either-or" which is not at all Christian. The event of the New Creation is interior to history precisely because it transcends it. It is because God is God that He has become man in Christ; and it is because God comes as man that man cannot really be himself unless he is deified. The incarnation of God and the deification of man are one and the same event, that of the New Creation.

6. From here we must consider another truth which we are apt to deform, or completely forget, as a result of the many crises we are now living through: the truth that the New Creation is lived within the Church. In this seventh vision (Rev 21-22), the central reality is the new Jerusalem. Without having to accept the two-book hypothesis defended by certain exegetes, we can simply see in the two readings of 21:1-8 and 21:9-15 the double perspective which is thoroughly characteristic of the prophets and writers of apocalyptic literature: the immediate future and the distant future. The two levels are not super-imposed on each other, but are rather interior to each other. The first vision of Jerusalem is no more heavenly than the second; the second is no more messianic than the first. Jerusalem is new precisely because transcendence is interior to it. The supreme Hour has arrived with the Pascha of the Lord. The Church is the figure and the sign of the Kingdom of God because the Kingdom is inaugurated now, within the life of the Church.

But in what way does the Church, seen in faith, and the Kingdom, mysteriously and humbly inaugurated right from this present moment, become the locus from which springs forth the event of the New Creation? A reading of verses 3-4 that immediately precede our text gives us the answer, if we set them in their larger biblical context, including especially Ezekiel 37:26f (cf. Isaiah 7:14). "I will make a covenant of peace with them . . . My dwelling place shall be with them; and I will be their God and they shall be my people . . . when my sanctuary is in the midst of them for evermore." This is the mystery of the temple and of the covenant which Jesus-Emmanuel has accomplished in His own person and which transfigures Jerusalem. The event of the New Creation is thus the event of the covenant. Yahweh is there in the heart of His people; the Spirit is there in the heart of the bride. The blood of the Lamb has sealed it, making of it a covenant that nothing can break, not even the infidelities of the bride of the Song of Songs. He delivered Himself for the Church, and He no longer belongs to Himself, but to His Church. Nor does the Church belong to itself, for it is only its true self insofar as it belongs to its Lord. The New Creation is the Creation of love that conquers death.

This new covenant constitutes the Church and gives it its reason for being. The eschatological meaning of our baptism is often neglected by Christians today. This sacrament renews us and brings us into the communion of the Church. This awareness should lead us, in our inter-Church relations, to recenter everything on the Church as the great sacrament, and to search all the more vigorously for ways to overcome the divisions which still exist in our communion of faith. This baptismal awareness should also lead us to live out more truly and more pointedly the tension between the two levels of time we spoke about earlier. Renewal of Christian ascetical practice depends in large part on our eschatological understanding of baptism. Renewal of our solidarity with all mankind also depends on this:

firstly, because the New Creation of and in the Church would be more acutely lived out as both transcendent to an interior to the world; and secondly, because the mysterious reality of which the Church is the sign—agape, divine *koinonia* or communion—would be perceived by our contemporaries as an active force, a force with the purity and power of the Gospel.

It is up to us whether the New Creation remains hidden and meaningless, or whether it deifies man and transfigures the world. Such is our responsibility in the present quest for authentic renewal.

CHAPTER 2

Renewal Today

To what kind of renewal is the Spirit calling the Churches in our time? A reading of Revelation 2-3 will be particularly helpful to us in answering this question.

1. One of the first signposts of that renewal concerns the very meaning of theology today. Every Christian is a theologian from the moment he has "loved the Epiphany," the *parousia* or appearance of Christ (2. Tm 4:8). The Christian's loving knowledge of the loving God is real, and it is centered on Him who comes into our world. The New Creation, as we have pointed out, shows itself not in the past, but in the coming future. It therefore follows that authentic theology is polarized by the coming of Christ. Now, far too often research that is called "theological" is nothing but a simple commentary on the past. We are not in any way advocating some fictional "theology" here; rather we wish to propose a *prophetic theology* that knows how to perceive the Coming of the Lord in history. Christians are often criticized for being behind the times in relation to the evolution of the modern world. It is not, however, a sociological or anthropological up-dating of our churches that will remedy our

present situation, but rather a true theological renewal. Instead of interpreting events in the light of the Bible after they have already happened, we ought to behold Him who comes into the world while we live out those events. And we should not merely perceive Him who comes, but we should also assist Him by making His coming easier. To hasten the coming of the creative Word, of Christ the Savior, is this not the goal toward which the Holy Spirit is leading us? Is He not striving to "lead us into all the truth," precisely because it is He who "announces to us the things to come?" (Jn 16:13).

Everything has already begun, and everything always begins anew for the Church, with the resurrection of our Lord. It was at the time of the resurrection that the Church recognized Jesus to be the "living one" (Rev 1:17-18), and thereby became the Church. The Church is the new humanity, a new humanity that from this present moment is given knowledge of the Lord of history. This kenosis, or self-emptying (Phil 2:7), is the eschatological condition of the Kingdom, and consequently of the theology which is the life of the Church in these final times. Theology has its source in this, that Christ is truly resurrected and has penetrated the veil of the first creation. Our renewal will be profoundly theological; or else it will be merely a re-adaption of an already outmoded past. Renewal within the Church occurs only through a profound penetration into the Mystery that works the second level of history, the interior reality, phenomena lead only to death.

True theology entails clear perception or knowledge of God in faith that leads to a clear perception of the world as both dialogical and diabolical as well as paschal and parousial. Without such a perception, there can be no renewal of theology.

2. We must recognize that Christian Newness, the reality of the New Creation, must be given an anthropological foundation and framework. If this is lacking today, it is partly due to the false dichotomy, denounced above, between conceptual transcendence and phenomenological immanence. The true tension as we have seen, is in fact eschatological. This does not mean that the Church should become an anthropological, sociological, or economic agency. A theological perspective neither destroys nor neglects the physical dimension of the person, rather, it penetrates to the sources of the psyche and liberates it. The Holy Spirit is not some super-psychology; He is the very life of the whole person. In the same way, a theological perspective does not eliminate the urgent need to know about the structures of human experience. It does however, elicit and transfigure the values which interact with those structures. The awareness of mystery, the "love of the parousia" which the Spirit kindles in the hearts of the baptized, is not reducible to any "religious experience," psychologizing sociology or structuralism. The mystery is the New Creation which penetrates into each of these domains to pull them out of the grave and lead them onwards towards the new heaven and the new earth.

This awareness is a revelation. If we are not a revelation for our brothers and sisters, surprising or irritating them as a sign of the "fall and rising," it is because we ourselves have fallen away from this fundamental awareness. As a result, we are only theists, and we should not be surprised that we have given birth to atheism. The primary question our world poses coincides with our first and most fundamental awareness as Christians: the question is not "Does God exist?"; it is not even "What is man?"; it is rather "How can man conquer death?", which comes down to the more basic question still, "Did Christ really rise from the dead?"

3. Such concerns demand a radical renewal in our churches. We have often transformed the dwelling of God with men into a den of thieves. We want to purify it, but we do not do that by "re-forming" the Church: it is not from us that the event of the New Creation springs forth. The Church is something given to us; it comes from God. But what are we doing with this gift? This is the real question. The focus of this must be upon Divine Communion given to men in Christ and spread abroad by the Spirit; for the Church is in the service of *agapê*. Everything that does not labor in this service merely expresses the dead and deadening character of the letter.

One of the most urgent renewals seems to me to be found in the area of the Church's spiritual gifts, to the extent that they have deviated from *agapê*. These gifts, or *charismata,* are the instrument of the New Creation in the Spirit that manifest the coming of this New Creation for the good of all men (1 Cor 12:7). If we read attentively what St Paul tells us at the end of 1 Cor 12 (vs. 27-28), we shall be in a position to revise the priorities that determine the state we find ourselves in. "First, apostles": the apostolic churches live on the sacramentality of this *charisma.* "Second, prophets . . .": where indeed is prophecy in our churches today? "Third, teachers": there is something of a glut on the market in this area today. . . . We could go on, noting that the *charisma* of governing comes nearly last, just before that of tongues: here again, what does this say about the present state of our churches?

In 1 Corinthians and elsewhere, Paul does not claim to give an exhaustive list of *charismata*. What forms would these *charismata* have to take really to translate and serve the New Creation which is coming into our world? The *charisma* of reconciliation seems to be one of the most urgent ones. Dialogue in fraternal and disinterested service is difficult to realize in certain parts of our world. There is also the supreme parousial *charisma* that Paul and the Fathers call "virginity" and which we call the "monastic life," for lack of a better term. It is a life whose meaning is bestowed by the inbreaking of the Parousia into our own historical order. Do our churches take these *charismata* seriously?

4. Confronted as we are by contemporary social, cultural, and personal events, we need an abundance of discernment. We dare yield neither to simple pragmatism nor to fantasy. But we must first of all operate within our eschatological perspective so that we can live out these contemporary events in a truly "new" way, according to the Christian meaning of the New Creation. The solution to our contemporary problems will thus be oriented theologically in the direction of true Christian theology.

5. In inter-ecclesial relationships, this same eschatological awareness can inject a new vigor into our dialogue. What is the best way to regulate contentious doctrinal or pastoral problems which still block full communion? Is it not to turn ourselves toward the Lord who is coming into the word? There is no pragmatic sentimentalism here, but rather the same certainty of

faith that would allow us to focus upon the heart of the Mystery. The dialogue between the churches is perhaps stuck in the period preceding Isaiah 43:19 in which people were still dreaming of "former things." Now it is certain that the Lord—"who is already appearing, can you not see him?"—is already making things new.

It would also help if we distinguished more clearly between the structures of the Church and its organization. In the final analysis, there are really only sacramental structures in the Church: constituted by the Holy Spirit as permanent signs and energies of the coming of the Lord. The Church is essentially sacramental because the Lord is not outside or beyond this world, but he is continually entering into it. Organization on the other hand, comes from us. It is no doubt necessary, in the service of agapê, but it is historically contingent. In itself, it is not the New Creation. The Church is not an objective order that can be studied and analyzed by the empirical tools of the sociologist. It is a power of creation, an organ of the Holy Spirit. It is in this sense, at this sacramental level, that the Church is given its structure.

6.   The relationship of the Church to the world is too often viewed from the exclusive viewpoint of organization, as though they represented two systems working in either mutual harmony or opposition. This relationship should instead be lived out in the meeting between divine Communion, made available in the Church by its sacramental structures, and the structures of this world that are animated by certain values. It is on the level of values that we have to live out the drama of Pascha and the Second Coming, to give life to what

is held captive by death. For it is only there that the New Creation can truly become manifest.

The mission of the Church in the modern world is not to be the bearer of techniques: the New Creation of the parousia does not introduce any new structures into the world. The mission of certain churches can and must be to offer material aid, "in deed and in truth" (1 Jn 3:18). But the mission of all the churches, rich or poor according to the criteria of this world, is to be the living and prophetic conscience of the world in our time. "The creation groans in birth-pains" (Rom 8:22); do we not know that? It is a clear assumption of St Paul. Do we live it? How do we translate it in the experience of work, money, matter and the cosmos?

7.   It seems clear that we must orient our research concerning ethical problems and liturgical renewal according to this profoundly eschatological perspective. The cultural revolution in which these two problems, ethical and liturgical are posed, a radical renewal, not only on the level of forms, which in themselves are contingent, but also and especially on the level of the Spirit. Culture, seen in the light of the parousia, is authentic iconography; it is the work of the Holy Spirit, who is even now "fashioning" Christ, the new Universe, out of the former creation.

"Behold, I make all things new": This implies no *deus ex machina,* that will produce some new arrangement of the cosmos. It signifies rather the beginning of the transformation of the sacramental liturgy into the eternal Liturgy. What will disappear is not this world, this marvel of the creative Word, but rather death itself. The New Creation will not mean the destruction of many generations of human accomplishments, but its definitive transfiguration, brought about by the ultimate *epiklesis* of the Holy Spirit.

PART TWO

Resurrection:
Its Significance For
Modern Man

Prologue

In the preceding chapters we have raised several linguistic and exegetical questions that the Mystery of the Resurrection poses to the conscience both of "modern man" and of Christian believers. In the present chapter, we want to investigate this same mystery as it relates to personal, social and political problems that we encounter in our world today—a world caught up in revolution.

Our investigation will be divided into four stages. In the first, even if such an approach is not satisfactory, we shall not raise the question: "What does the Resurrection mean for us today?" Rather, we shall ask: why do we even raise the question? If we really want to better understand the meaning of the Resurrection for our life in the modern world, it seems preferable to begin, not with what the Resurrection means in and of itself, but rather with the meaning of our inquiry about it: "Why does the Resurrection pose a question for us today?"

By beginning in this way, we will situate ourselves on the level of our own experience, and then, at a second stage, we will be better prepared to recognize the real meaning of the Mystery of the Resurrection in terms of what it was once and for all, and of what it continues to mean for Christ Himself. The third stage of our investigation will consist of a personal meeting between the event of the Resurrection and our own life, a meeting that will take place on a truly personal level. Modern problems concerning the meaning of "person" are sufficiently numerous and complex as to justify our devoting a separate chapter to them. Without at all falling into individualism or a false familiarity, we must recognize that all of our questions concern the person and the human conscience, including those questions that deal with social and political concerns.

Only in a fourth stage, therefore, will we be able to clarify the relationship that exists between the Mystery of the Resurrection and the social-political problems of our world. In this regard, we will be concerned not only with the meeting, but even more with a kind of "spiritual" reading of the event of the Resurrection itself. From this perspective, we will find ourselves forced to ask, not if the Resurrection has meaning in our life, but does our life not rather discover its meaning in the Resurrection.

But let's not get ahead of ourselves. First of all we have to raise the basic question: why do we even find ourselves today obliged to raise the question of the meaning of the Resurrection in our life?

CHAPTER 1

Why This Question?

This question itself should surprise us. A critical perspective precedes and accompanies every authentic vision of faith. Well then, let's be critical! The question itself is a fact; yet it is a surprising fact. At a certain moment in history, some people at Antioch were given the name "christians" by other people. For the so-called "christians," Christ is alive and He constitutes their very life. For the others, this Christ lived at a given moment, and then He died and was buried; and the "christians" are simply His disciples. For the "christians" themselves, the Resurrection of this Christ is an obvious fact that gives meaning to their entire life. For the others, this same Resurrection is only a word devoid of meaning. The same contrast is to be found during the trial of St Paul at Caesarea before Festus, Agrippa and Bernice. The Roman well understood the conflict that set the Jews against Paul: "They had certain points of dispute with him about their own superstition and about one Jesus, who was dead, but whom Paul asserted to be alive" (Acts 25:19).

For whom does the Resurrection pose a question? For Paul? But the Resurrection is both the affirmation

53

and the witness of his entire life. For the Jews? Yes, because they affirm the reality of death, and want to leave it at that. And also for the governor, who very honestly admits to "being at a loss how to investigate these matters" (Acts 25:20). As for ourselves, with whom do we identify in asking ourselves the meaning of the Resurrection for our life today? With these "christians" of Antioch, or with Paul, or with the sceptical Jews, or with the honest and embarrassed Roman? Without any doubt, we identify a little bit with each one of them. But why?

a) A first series of feelings or motivations rises up within us because of the scepticism of the Jews and the embarrassment of Festus. Let's try to analyze them. It is perhaps somewhat delicate for me, an Orthodox from Antioch, to venture into such an analysis, but I shall try to do so in a spirit of peace and fraternal love. The imperceived underlying facts of the question that concerns us are of course very closely linked to the well-perceived history of the Western Church that began in the early fifth century. In this history of the Latin Church, both Catholics and Protestants belong to the same cultural and religious world. Now the question that we have to raise is a typical product of that world.

It appears quite clear that the past history of the Western Church was particularly sensitive to the suffering involved in the Passion of Christ. From sculptured representations of the Cross to the liturgical expression of Easter, the historical realism of the suffering and death of Jesus is especially evident. This sensitivity is particularly keyed in to chronology and events, and in this regard it is faithful to the literal meaning of the

Gospel accounts. And yet from this perspective, it is the Cross that captures the full attention of the Christian mind. The Resurrection only comes afterwards (chronologically), it is not represented over and above the image of the Empty Tomb, and very little is said of it in the Gospels. Until the last few years at least, Western Christian piety disassociated Cross and Resurrection and concentrated almost exclusively upon the Cross. As evidence, it's sufficient to take a look at the hymnals and prayer books of some thirty years ago, many of which are still in use.

This first approach to liturgical prayer, in which the Church lives its faith, is confirmed by the approach of theological thought, in which the Church reflects upon its faith. A constant theme is evident throughout Western theology, from Augustine of Hippo to Anselm of Canterbury, and from the theologians of the Reform and Counter-Reform to those of today. This theme can be described as that of the "isolated man," man conceived in himself, separated from other men. It is in essence a profoundly pessimistic theme. Above all, the Manichaeism of Augustine left from the beginning a deep mark upon medieval and modern Latin theology. From that point on, there have been periodic repetitions, like those of a scratched record: man as sinner, nature and grace, justification, grace alone or pure nature, and finally the manifold atheism of today that reacts against such themes by rejecting them out of hand as meaningless. At the heart of this theological perspective, the Resurrection remains totally secondary, considered as an unessential and marginal issue.

Without resorting to computers, it would be inter-

esting to determine the frequency and importance of
the theme of the Resurrection in the courses and hand-
books that have educated future pastors in various
schools of theology. We can say without exaggeration,
until the last few years, the theme of Resurrection-
Ascension was simply included as a final chapter of the
doctrine of Redemption. It was regarded as a kind of
brief appendix that concluded endless discussions about
the means of Redemption, the notions of satisfaction
and the Cross, and the themes of sin and justification.
Moreover, the most common form of this meager chapter on the Resurrection was that of "apologetic": the
Empty Tomb, for example, was presented as the irre-
futable proof that Christ is God and that His teaching
is authentic. Given these factors, it becomes clear that
our motives in raising the question of the meaning of
the Resurrection for our life are especially positive
ones. We want to know just what the Resurrection can
possibly mean in our life in an age in which
Augustinian and Lutheran anthropology and anti-
modernist apologetic no longer interest us.

Another fact contributes significantly to our question: the chronic lack of an adequate doctrine of the
Holy Spirit in Latin theology. Modern theologians are
sufficiently aware of the problem to justify our mentioning it. Nevertheless, I shall draw only one conclusion from it, one that from an Orthodox point of view
seems perfectly obvious. Insofar as the role of the Holy
Spirit is inadequately perceived in the event of the
Mystery of the Resurrection, the inevitable consequence
is that the Resurrection of Christ remains simply and
solely an event of the past. As a result, the more we
are removed in time from the initial event, the less that

event bears any influence on our actual existence. As cultural factors intervene, influenced by modern historical criticism and Biblical interpretation, the concept of the Resurrection becomes so fragmented that each interpreter preserves of it only what he wants: either he limits it to the historical phenomenon, reduced to a minimum by modern criticism, or else he derives from it the illusion that faith can be "liberated" from history.

As we shall see farther on, it is only the Holy Spirit who enables us to enter into the realism of the Mystery. But what is a shame in this regard, is the fact that the cultural conditioning of Western theology makes Christians allergic to "spiritual realism." It is not my intention to discuss here in detail the various reasons for this cultural conditioning. Permit me simply to mention them briefly. Modern man—or more accurately, his vision inspired by the American and European values that hold sway over the world—is obsessed to the point of myopia by the analysis and mastery of observable phenomena. Beyond this superficial exterior where everything can be reduced to sheer quantity, nothing exists that has any real value.

Even on the privileged level of this Western culture, this allergy to spiritual realism is reinforced by a certain tendency to think in terms of the dichotomy "phenomenon/technique." The most striking example is perhaps the impasse that has been reached in our era concerning economic and social development, an impasse roundly denounced by the revolutionary events of 1968. The ideologies of technical progress on the one hand and of social progress on the other have come into conflict for the past fifty years, each defending the same ideal of the liberation of man. And still, humanity is no less alienated today than it was then. By focusing our attention on only one aspect of man's life, we have forgotten man himself. This maniacal dichotomizing has led us back to the overworked theme of nature and grace, even if the words have changed and nature has been dethroned by anthropology and sociology. In this world closed in upon itself, it is quite evident that no perspective opens onto the Resurrection. But it's rather ironic that the only protest to this, based upon experience rather than upon a particular idealism, is heard from Soviet philosophers of science-fiction. They alone dare speak of "geophobia" and of human aspiration towards an "encounter" in "another realm" that will bring about man's fulfillment.

Certainly we cannot look to this source for any real answers. In fact, we can detect in these writers another engaging theme that powerfully conditions both culture and the "new theology": I'm speaking of messianic compensations. The Revelation of St John had already warned us of the manifold messianism that would appear in successive waves throughout history. Our own century is a past master in the art of changing costumes. Ideologies succeed one another without even the time to express themselves in terms of a philosophy; and soon we'll have to discover a word to replace the term "revolution," a term that is already as shopworn and disappointing as the term "progress." Not that everything in this travesty is a sheer lie; far from it. The problem of hunger, for example, has been seriously dealt with. Nevertheless hunger remains: a true spiritual hunger.

Add to that a passionate hermeneutic that seeks "meaning," such as structuralism, employed as a scientific method rather than as a system, and deals essentially with all that is superficial. Add as well a serious pastoral anxiety, without precedent in the history of the Church, that suffers from the fact that attention is paid almost exclusively to the emotional weight of the message and not enough to its vital content. Then finally, consider the tragic mocking that greets the heart of the Christian Mystery, due especially to its past psychological blocks created by the provisional character of Church institutions and the changes presently taking place in those institutions. Taking all these factors into consideration leads us almost to the end of the first series of feelings or motivations that oblige us to raise the question: "What does the Resurrection mean for modern man?" To tell the truth, these feelings or motivations in fact do much to cloud the question and anesthetize the hunger that leads us to raise it in the first place. Nonetheless, it was necessary for us to consider them for a moment, not only to be able to recognize them at a later stage of our inquiry, but also to enable us to perceive another chain of motivations that reflect fundamental and inevitable questions dealing with the most basic issues of life. It is these motivations that take us to the threshold of our encounter with the Mystery of the Resurrection.

b) This second series of feelings or motivations shares the common characteristic of coming forth from life and being authenticated by life, despite interference from the first series. They concern our most vital aspirations, and they cannot be contained within a system. Cultural conditioning can disguise them, but it cannot eliminate them. At times technology and the marketing of ideas can alienate them; but sooner or later they will break free to set man squarely before his true problems. We can summarize these aspirations by referring to a specific fact: our confrontation with death. For these feelings and motivations invariably proceed from death, and in one way or another they eventually return to death. Man is able to live, and the modern consciousness is certainly more lucid concerning everything that poses a threat to life. Without doubt, that is why the first series of motivations is so powerful today. It amounts to a kind of over-compensation by which man seeks to prove to himself that he is capable of overcoming the power of death.

We will have an opportunity to come back to this subject when we consider our personal, social and political problems. What we should underscore here is the way in which these vital aspirations actually brave death today and thereby lead us to raise in the most urgent way our original question concerning the meaning of the Resurrection.

On the one hand, we can recognize the deep concern for authenticity—indeed, for absolute sincerity—that drives modern man. In this regard, it is quite possible that believers of earlier generations were less inclined to reflect upon the actual influence of the Resurrection in their lives, limited as they were by a whole network of constraints and habits. They were assured of a certain spiritual equilibrium, but often at the price of an unconscious absence of truth. Today, on the other hand, when social appearances and constraints are easily unmasked, we can no longer exorcise death by means of alibis. We must deal with it as it is. But this means that we cannot avoid raising the question of the present and efficient meaning of the Resurrection.

In the same line of thought, we should mention the problem of existential meaning to which the modern consciousness is gradually returning after its long intoxication with nominalism, idealism, and their consequences. To an age of faith, when that Truth which is Life was reduced to a religious rationalism and finally to a vague "belief," there is substituted today the requirement of verification through experience. We sense in a confused way that everything that remains in the sphere of ideas, and has not yet taken concrete form in the sphere of existence, bears the mark of death. This perspective leads to a double criticism of religious thought. On the one hand, we reject as some idealistic superstructure everything that is not truly efficient in life; and on the other, we are better prepared to accept that which can truly transform life. If we apply this double perspective to the Mystery of the Resurrection, we can well understand that the modern consciousness should be sceptical about its meaning, if it is nothing more than an event of the past or a simple moral example. And we can also understand that today we are perhaps better prepared to experience the transforming power of the Resurrection, since in fact it marks the great explosion of Life into our world of death.

I would like to see another element injected into the growing concern of the modern conscience, namely a sense for "global" meaning. We are all aware of the diverse socio-cultural factors that have come together to give 20th century man his global perception of existence. The fact is that we sense much better than our ancestors did the interplay and interdependence of every level of the human tragedy. The result is that we have become suspicious of any partial solution to the problems of life, and consequently we are irresistibly seduced by every apparently global solution to the difficulties of our existence. That is why ideologies have replaced philosophies, because the former, less developed but more ambitious, offer to man a "totalitarian" explanation of history. The application of this concern to the Resurrection is clear. Either the Resurrection of Christ is a partial truth, one among many others, perceived by a few visionaries, and consequently it holds no *a priori* interest for modern man; or else it is the global Truth itself, that Reality which "verifies" all things and thereby bestows its own meaning upon all things. It is evident that this way of approaching the question, characteristic of the modern soul, leads us to the point of understanding St Paul's audacious affirmation: "If Christ has not been raised, then our preaching is in vain and your faith is in vain . . . we are of all men the most to be pitied" (1 Cor 15:14, 19).

Unfortunately, there are few people who have the courage to follow this existential logic to its natural conclusion. Rare are those who, day after day, dare to verify the terrible statement of Albert Camus: "There is only one serious philosophical problem: suicide." Whether we like it or not, whether we are conscious of it or not, we can never escape the implacable dilemma of every minute of our existence: either to commit suicide or to rise from the dead.

We shall return to these questions in the third part of this essay. I simply wanted to raise the issue at this point in response to the serious nature of our modern quest for meaning. We should in fact throw out all together every ideology and every religion, including every form of decadent Christianity, insofar as they do not enable us to live out a global solution to our existence. The most serious vice of every ideology and religion is to disregard the only truly essential question of life, namely the question of death. In all honesty, I as a modern man can only accept as a global and meaningful explanation of my life and of history an explanation that allows me here and now to confront and to go beyond the tragedy of death. Apart from such an explanation there is nothing but distraction and lies.

We need not recall here the role of derision in contemporary literature and film, but this cultural symptom is indicative of a mentality that reveals a terrible truth. In the face of the dilemma of "suicide or resurrection," if the term "Resurrection" is nothing more than an empty word that most people totally ignore, then human consciousness is left with only one honest explanation to things, namely, that they are absurd. This means, of course, that ultimately existence is devoid of any explanation and of all meaning. The only meaning of existence is that there is none. What a strange end for *homo faber* and *homo technicus!* He can explain everything except himself, for the ultimate affirmation about himself is that there is nothing at all to affirm! For if man has no meaning, nothing that he does has any meaning either. If that is the case, let's simply blow our brains out right now. Or better, let's render the ultimate service to humanity and blow up the planet as well, before any of us feel tempted to emigrate to somewhere else in the universe. Let us push "geophobia" to its logical conclusion, and without a trace of dark humor, let us recognize that the only serious fighters for a cause are the anarchists. For it is not any particular structure that must be done away with, but rather the sturcture of things taken as a whole; for us, structure in and of itself has the power to give life to mankind. Revolution or conservatism are only variations on the same deadly boring theme: the dance of death . . . All of this is the tragic condition of those who are untouched by the preaching of the Gospel. Nevertheless, our era seems to be on the threshold of that Gospel. This is obvious to anyone who has "beheld" the risen Lord, the Lord who is coming into our world with power. There is dramatic truth in the affirmation that "we are waiting for the resurrection of the dead." For we ourselves are those dead. Still, it is equally true that we cannot offer ourselves that Resurrection. For it is utterly beyond us—and yet it is absolutely essential to our life.

In order to complete this second series of feelings or motivations that lead modern man to seek with increasing honesty the true meaning of Resurrection in his life, we should mention the diverse forms of renewal taking place in the various Churches that make such a quest possible. Permit me simply to make note of them without going into detail.

These renewal movements are by no means limited to the revived interest in forgotten subjects such as patristic studies, the history of liturgies or the vast field of Biblical science. I am thinking rather of the major factors that bear witness to the activity of the Holy Spirit, who today is in the process of filling and renewing the people of God. For example, the concern of many Christian people today to enter into a living, existential relationship with the Word of God is evidently the fruit of the rediscovery of the "spiritual sense" of the Word as He is incarnated and resurrected in our life. This concern goes well beyond a fundamentalist biblical literalism that has amply demonstrated its inability to serve as a life-giving force. A similar renewal is needed on the level of liturgical renewal in the West. This requires a sense of realism in our evaluation of what has already occurred in this regard, since the components of that renewal are also subject to a certain literalism and can be just as deadening as the letter of the Scriptures. No, our quest is for something other than that; something that corresponds to the "spiritual realism" that we spoke of earlier and that stands at the very heart of our Christian experience of Resurrection. Finally, we can mention the patient rediscovery of an authentically Christian anthropology, together with (to the degree that certain theologians refrain from boycotting Eastern tradition) a heightened sensitivity to the renewing power of the Holy Spirit within man.

Having sketched out these various motivations, and discovered their points of convergence, we are now in a position to recognize all the more clearly the significance of the Resurrection event itself, lived once for all by our Lord and experienced as a life-giving power throughout human history.

CHAPTER 2

The Mystery of the Resurrection

According to a certain human logic, we should begin by asking ourselves about the meaning of death, in order then to understand the meaning of "resurrection"; that is, if it is true that to "rise from the dead" means to come to life again after having once been dead. I dare put forth this elementary observation so that we can better grasp its ambiguity, indeed its sheer senselessness. This sort of approach would be pointless in the first place because in fact death *has* no meaning: it is pure absurdity, the very essence of non-meaning. Within the light of the resurrected Christ, we understand that no death has "meaning" or positive significance other than that which is beyond death, in the life that the reality of death both hides and reveals, giving us access to it. This awareness can be ours, however, only from within the event of the Lord's Resurrection. Therefore we will begin with the Resurrection itself, and only then will we ask the question, "Death, where is your victory?"

The approach that would begin by asking the "meaning" of death is inane for another reason, for it presupposes a confusion that is wide-spread today concerning the meaning of the term "resurrection." This mysterious word is all too often used in the limited sense of "to come back to life." The crucial point, however, is that the Resurrection of Christ does not involve the simple reanimation of a dead body. It is something wholly different from the resuscitation of Lazarus; it is, in fact, unique. We cannot grasp the meaning of Jesus' Resurrection by taking as our starting point His physical death. To the contrary, the death of Jesus of Nazareth only has meaning in the light of His Resurrection. Only Christ's Resurrection can explain what led up to it and what followed it, including the very mystery of death in which we find ourselves involved at every moment. If death remains the inexplicable enigma whose absurdity strips away all meaning from our own existence and that of humanity as a whole, the Resurrection of Christ stands as the unique event that bestows its universal Truth upon all that exists.

History, whether personal, communal or cosmic, is a sealed book that only the Lamb can open: the Lamb who is "slain" (for He truly died; His death is a fact), yet who is "standing" (for He is truly risen from the dead; His Resurrection is also a fact, albeit one of a different order), as the Apocalypse affirms (Rev 5:5-6). If our quest for the meaning of Resurrection depends only on simple human logic, then it will fall far short of its goal. It must be guided and illumined by a new and different light, the light of Revelation. The Resurrection of Christ is in fact the ultimate Revelation, the ultimate "apocalypse." "Fear not; I am the first and the last, and the living one. I died, and behold I am alive for evermore, and I have the Keys of Death and Hades" (Rev 1:17f).

We should stress once again the fact that the Resurrection of Christ is not an event like any other, on the order of historical phenomena that can be investigated by the media. From a superficial point of view, this is what distinguishes it from Christ's Passion, an "event" about which we have very precise and detailed accounts. No hidden witness inside the tomb could have taken a photo of the event of the Resurrection! On the other hand, any contemporary reporter could have filmed Lazarus as he came forth from the tomb. No, the Resurrection of Christ is no ordinary event that can be analyzed by scientific methods; nevertheless, it is an historical fact, a true event that occurred in the course of our history and vitally concerns our history. We can even say that the Resurrection is in the image of the true and living God. Although not an ordinary event, it is nonetheless the most *real* event of all times.

In Biblical terms, we could say that the Resurrection is not a "flesh and blood" event, but rather an event of the Kingdom of God, that Kingdom which dwells both among and within us. The Body of Christ that rises from the dead is truly a Body; it is a living Body; it is a living Body—St Paul would say, "a spiritual Body," filled with the Breath of God, the divine *Pneuma* that knows nothing of death.

Without repudiating our exegetical approaches to the question, we can nevertheless understand the discretion of the Evangelists who refuse to describe the Lord's Resurrection, while they devote the most important part of their testimony to His Passion. The fact that Jesus suffered and died is a reality seen and known by everyone who was present. It was a concrete fact, even if its meaning escaped most of those who witnessed it. The Resurrection is also a fact; it is, however, a mystery: the extraordinary Mystery of God and man that no longer contains the ambiguity inherent in the interpretation of ordinary phenomena. Either it remains unknown and inaccessible, or else it is radiant with meaning. To be more precise, it is not an "event" in and of itself, concrete, capable of being isolated and analyzed by subsequent investigation that could only interpret it and explain its meaning in a remote and exterior way. To the contrary, it is the purest form of "relational event," relating with all that is inseparable from creation and from the Creator, illumining all things from within and giving meaning to all, since it is both the origin and the end of all.

Christ, the Son of the living God and of the Virgin Mary, rises from the dead, not by some inner principle of superior biological evolution (after all, the world as a whole still dwells in death), but by the fresh and creative intervention of the living God. Paradoxically, the Resurrection is an inbreaking of "discontinuity" into our world—and as such, it brings about genuine "continuity." It means discontinuity because it utterly surpasses human power and capacity; yet it brings about the fullness of continuity because finally, in Christ, man becomes a truly living being. By His Resurrection, Christ magnificently fulfills His own word: "I have not come to abolish, but to fulfill."

Moreover, it is under this sign of fulfillment that the Evangelists, and Luke in particular, reveal to us the mystery of the Resurrection. Everything that goes before it finds its meaning only in the risen Christ. It is not possible to do so here, but it would be necessary to review each stage in the history of the Old Testament, in order to discover that all of it has meaning, especially as it concerns ourselves, only in the person of the risen Lord. The most basic insight of the apostolic kerygma consisted in demonstrating, above all to the children of Israel, that the fulfillment of salvation history has occurred in and through the Resurrection. Perhaps it is because we have lost the vitality of the apostolic preaching that we no longer perceive just how all this long history leading up to the Paschal event has meaning for ourselves as well, insofar as it is illumined by the central event of the Resurrection.

Let us nonetheless briefly go over these major stages of Old Testament history, for we will soon find them again in our own personal and social history, since they provide us with the main outline of the whole human drama. The creation, that great gift of life from the living God, is brought to conclusion in the Resurrection, the definitive victory over all death. The promise made to Abraham is fulfilled in the Resurrection (Acts 13:32), offering mankind the true gift of the Son, the new People and the new Land. The Passover, prefigured with Moses, is truly realized only in the "passage" or passing over from death to life of the first born Son together with his brothers and sisters. The exodus only has meaning in its fulfillment in the risen Christ. He is the living Way, the living Bread, and His Spirit is the source of living water. The covenant, as we shall see, is only new and eternal in the Resurrection: He becomes our God and we become His people. The Kingdom is nothing other than the glorified Body of the risen Christ, in which each day humanity enters into communion. The drama of the exile, brought to completion on the Cross, would be absurd if it were not the final crumbling away of every boundary and limit in which human idolatry seeks constantly to imprison the God of all mankind. In the risen Christ, the exile becomes the true return to the true land where we find all men brought together, beyond barriers of language, race, nation and religion. Finally, the true restoration of the Davidic dynasty and of the temple, never realized after the return from exile, is brought to completion in the body of the resurrected Christ. He is the true temple, the authentic dwelling place of God among men, from which salvation flows forth and where the Father is worshipped in Spirit and in truth.

Through all these stages in the history of salvation, a marvellously faithful plan is revealed; insofar as we read that history, we see it in the Bible and in our own lives, in the light of the Resurrection. For there we find the gift of life, from its first appearance until its full bloom. The Resurrection of Jesus is the manifestation, once and for all in the humanity assumed by the Son of God, of the mystery of life in the Holy Trinity. Starting from this moment, God begins to be all in all. The Resurrection is the beginning of the Parousia, the unfolding of the transparent revelation of God and of man.

What in fact is opposed to this communion in the light which is the ultimate good news (1 John 1:1-8), if not death? We shall discover the true Biblical meaning of death in the light of Christ. Let us say right away, however, that death is not primarily a matter of biological decomposition, for that is only its consequence. Death is fundamentally a rupture of communion, a missed relation (*khata'a* in Hebrew and Arabic, "to miss the goal"). It provokes a rupture between two beings who ought to be united. Everything else is a consequence of this mortal wound: sin, suffering, law . . . The Resurrection of Christ, then, is the event of salvation brought about by the living God, by which a man definitively pierced through the wall of death. Henceforth this Jesus, who is truly the Son of God and truly shares our humanity, is truly Man without any mortal limit. Space, time, the past and the future, superficiality of relationships and our absence from one another, all these marks of death can no longer touch Him and no longer hold Him in bondage. The risen Christ is the only man who is in present and perpetual communion with all beings. Just as the tomb could not retain His humanity, so the hardness of our hearts and the many obstacles that stand between us can no longer break the covenant of love that unites Him to us. He is God, present to everyone and to everything. As man, He is not only a living being; He has become a "life-giving Spirit" (1 Cor 15:45).

CHAPTER 3

"To Know Him and the Power of His Resurrection"

(Phil. 3:10)

In the second part of the preceding presentation, we recalled the first essential aspect of the mystery of the Resurrection as it was experienced once and for all by the Lord Himself. There we concluded with the words of Paul to the Corinthians (I Cor 15:45): "The last Adam became a life-giving Spirit." It would have been desirable to develop a bit more fully what the extraordinary event of being raised from the dead represented for Christ Himself. To do so, however, would have run the risk of deforming the mystery by considering it in and of itself, whereas we have already seen, the essence of the Resurrection is to be, not one event among others, but *the* event which contains all the others. It was by raising his Son from the dead that the Father realized his eternal design of "recapitulating" in Christ everything that exists (Eph 1:10). Let us be certain of one thing: despite all our nominalist and rationalist temptations, our God cannot be known as an "object," for then He would become an idol made by man, an idol that the literature on the "death of God" proclaims to be no more. Similarly, the Resurrection of the Lord is not a reality knowable in an "objective" way; it is, however, at the center of all relations that constitute what is truly real. "Recapitulate" is a term coined by Paul to mean "to bring together under one single head," "to restore a head" to that which was inorganic and disorganized. Without the Resurrection, the world becomes mere chaos. With the Resurrection, however, it becomes an organic "cosmos" and in very truth the "Body of Christ." This basic conviction, that the Resurrection is the masterpiece of God who "brought all things from nothingness into being," from darkness into light, from chaos into true "cosmos," will guide us in the two following areas of concern: that of our personal problems on the one hand, and of our social and political problems on the other.

What is the impact of the Resurrection on our personal experience, insofar as it is truly "personal"? First of all, let us eliminate all moral or superficial interpretations that would make the risen Christ the model, rooted in the past, of a new life in God. This kind of interpretation would destroy the mystery and plunge us once again into death. In fact, the essential meaning of the Resurrection of Jesus for the human person is one of a radically new existence. "The old has passed away, behold, the new has come!" (2 Cor 5:17). There is a real participation of our very humanity in the life of the living God. To be raised from the dead in Christ is to attain the ultimate stage in our spiritual growth: to become God by participation. This is one reason why, in the preceding section, I only partially developed the meaning of the Resurrection for the Lord Himself: for this meaning is in fact wholly relative to ourselves. But in what sense?

"He died for all, that those who live might live no longer for themselves but for Him who for their sake died and was raised." (2 Cor 5:15). We can find other such references in the Epistles, in particular this decisive statement from Romans: "You have died to the law through the Body of Christ, so that you may belong to another, to Him who has been raised from the dead in order that we may bear fruit for God" (Rom 7:4).

In recalling above the major stages in God's design as revealed in the Bible, we spoke of the fulfillment of the mystery of the Covenant through the Resurrection of Christ. This mystery of the Covenant stands at the heart of human history. It is the mystery of the Holy Trinity, for our God is Covenant, Love, Communion (*koinonia*). Through Jesus Christ, we are invited to participate in true life, eternal life that begins in the present moment. All the other stages in the economy of salvation converge toward this Covenant; just as in our ecclesial life all is centered on the eucharistic liturgy, the great sacrament of the Covenant in His Body and Blood; just as in our daily lives everything is "recapitulated" in *agapê,* the divine communion which brings all things together into unity. The Resurrection of Christ, then, is the total and definitive fulfillment of this Covenant, in which our God becomes totally "ours" and in which we become totally "His."

We no longer belong to ourselves but we belong to Christ. This is not a matter of some legal contract or moral ideal; it is a mysterious and spiritual reality that encompasses our whole being: body, mind, soul and

spirit. In the power of the Resurrection the whole of
humanity is snatched from death and given back to the
Father. In reality, on the level of our personal and
responsible participation, this mystery becomes "ours"
by faith and by the primary operative sign of that faith:
our baptism and unction by the Holy Spirit. We are
thus given a new being, a new ontological existence
which comes from God. This is the "spiritual realism"
we spoke about earlier. Our deified being in Christ is
not an ideology but a reality. This reality, however,
is not of "flesh and blood," but of the Holy Spirit, and
therefore it is "spiritual." In this regard, let us eliminate
right away any idealistic interpretation of the word
"spiritual." It does not mean "disincarnated," in opposition to the body or to matter; we are not Platonists or
Manicheans. The word "spiritual" means "animated by
the Breath of God," living in freedom from every form
of death; just as "carnal" in the Biblical sense does not
refer to what is biological or material, but to the condition of a living human being wounded by sin and death.

It is precisely this "flesh" that the Word of God
assumed so as to *liberate* it from sin and death. His
Resurrection is our victory and our liberation: our
whole being can thus begin to live according to the
Spirit, even in our present bodily condition. Our entire
history thus becomes a great Pascha, begun in the
heart of our being by the pouring forth of the Holy
Spirit and to be completed by the transfiguration of our
bodies (Rom 8:11 and Phil 3:21).

Obviously, this involves certain immediate consequences on the level of our moral conduct. The Pauline
letters are sufficiently eloquent on this subject, and we
need not dwell upon it. Let us be careful, however, not

to reduce the Christian mystery to a new moral code: our conduct "according to the Spirit," is the fruit of our essential rebirth. The root itself has changed. We have been grafted onto the living Christ (Rom 6:5); a new sap is running through our branches, and for this reason, we can bear the fruits of light. Henceforth we live "for God" because in truth we have been "deified."

This is the sum of the Christian kerygma: life has been manifested in Jesus Christ, the incarnate Word of God, and this life is communicated to us through His Death and Resurrection. But how does this life enter into us? The question of "meaning," which we have been asking all along, gives us the answer. I suggest that we contemplate a liturgical icon, that speaks far more eloquently and with far more power about our theological transformation than any scholarly treatise. I am referring to the icon of the Descent into Hell. In Byzantine tradition, this is the most faithful liturgical expression we possess of the mystery of Resurrection. Moreover, in this icon we have a precious indication of the authenticity of any given theological tradition. We are all familiar with the paintings, and even certain icons produced in times of decadence, that depict Christ rising out of the tomb. After what we have said about the mystery of the Resurrection, inaccessible as an historical phenomenon, we can sense the degradation of the faith which is visible in these representations. The Resurrection is not a visible event, representable in a graphic way, and certainly it cannot be represented "in itself," but only "for us." This is why the icon of the Descent into Hell is a liturgical sign that stands very much closer to the mystery than these other images. It draws us towards the inner meaning of the event and enables us to enter into a personal relationship with it.

The risen Christ, radiant with light, is the image of the invisible God in His transfigured humanity; He penetrates into the depths of our darkness to snatch man and woman from the tomb where death has held them as prisoners. The full dynamism of our new life is expressed here. "To know Him and the power of His Resurrection" (Phil 3:10) consists in this movement by which Christ descends into our very depths to raise us up into the light of Life. This is the movement of baptism, descent and rising up (Rom 6:3-4), with all the spiritual realism that the power of the Spirit will realize within us day after day in our personal lives.

Our present participation in the Resurrection of Christ consists in His descent into hell, that is, into our personal depths. Yet how can He transfer all things into the realm of light? Without confusing the Christian mystery with a systematized psychological science, or adopting some theory of psycho-spiritual harmony, we must nevertheless draw upon today's knowledge of man's make-up. In the same way, we find in St Paul's letters allusions to the anthropology of his time, yet we must be careful not to confuse this vision of man with the Christian revelation. Today we possess a relatively detailed knowledge concerning the psychic depths of man, whatever may be the underlying theory that seeks to systematize that knowledge.

What stands out in this regard is the fact that the human personality is made up of various levels or stages, four-fifths of which are unconscious. There is the organic self, the social self or person, the conscious self, the unconscious self and the "super-ego." Each of these levels expresses an aspect of the personality: its bio-social solidarity, its need for security, its need to be part of a group, its search for value, its interiority, and its moral regulation. In this bundle of needs and poten-tialities, which are often without any order and difficult to coordinate, we are looking for ways to bring about some kind of unity within ourselves, polarized as we are by the world of false values. I will not go into detail in this analysis; permit me simply to restate the ques-tion: What is the impact of the Lord's Resurrection on this deepest level of personal life?

The first reality experienced by the baptized Chris-tian is that all this human richness is brought again into the light. The Holy Spirit truly works within the depths of the various levels of our personality. First of all, we come to appreciate that "all of that is good." The Resurrection makes us aware of the fundamental well-being of the creation. It also becomes clear that all this that is good exists for the sake of relationships with others rather than to be turned in on itself. In a very realistic way, this permits the basic traits of the image of God to manifest themselves within our innermost being. It also becomes clear that the actualization—the "likeness"—of all this richness must go through a pro-cess of growth. Restoration of the divine likeness must proceed from the first creation to the Resurrection by passing through the stages of promise, passover and the other moments in the history of salvation that we spoke of earlier. These stages then begin to assume all of their present anthropological meaning. John wrote the prologue to his Gospel in the light of the glory of the Resurrection. Therefore he could declare that "the Word was the true light which enlightens every man . . .

and He became flesh ... and we have beheld his glory" (John 1:9, 14). What does our profession of faith signify when we affirm in the Creed that "He will return in glory?" This return is a present reality; it is the risen Christ who comes to us and already enables us to participate in His Glory. Here is where the mystery of the Cross receives its full significance, revealed in and through the Resurrection.

The Word of Light enters into us to enlighten our darknesses. "The life was the light of men, and the light shone in the darkness and the darkness could not overcome it" (John 1:4-5). The risen Christ reveals to us from within the true meaning of death. Death has no reality in and of itself, like one psychic element alongside another or a virus inside a living organism; it is rather a certain way of being that characterizes our very personality. Death is a broken relationship, an absence of light, a lack of communion: it is a rupture, an exile, a slavery . . . All the various Biblical images could be used here. True death, seen in the light of the Resurrection, is nothing other than sin: the solitude of man as the divine image who strives by every created thing to reach out toward the light of communion (1 John 1:5), yet falls again into his own darkness.

Psychologically, it would be easy to analyze our experience of death. We can give it the names of disappointment, failure, dispersion, anarchy, stagnation, regression, rupture, rejection . . . In fact, death is a certain form of relationship, or rather a lack of relationship. The Resurrection establishes us in a covenant-relation; it reconciles us, it justifies us, it leads us back into communion. This second stage in the descent into hell is thus the actual moment of salvation, in which the Word of Light enters into and assumes darkness (the Lamb assumes the sin of the world), and thereby He disperses the darkness, just as the rising sun disperses the shadows of the night. This does not occur without pain; it is a tragic event. Christ truly died. He fought against the very powers of darkness, not against myths. But because this man is the Son of the living God, death has been crushed in its own kingdom by the one it was holding captive. The finest theological expression of this paschal drama is surely to be found in our Easter liturgies, and it is to them that we should return again and again.

We must not forget, however, that we are not talking about a simple natural therapy, such as the best psychoanalysis could (and only rarely does) provide. Our redemption is our deification. The saving action carried out by the risen Christ is the greatest doxological work of all: the glory of God is man created anew or a living being. If Christ died and was raised for us, it was to enable us to live no longer for ourselves but for Him. This marvellous transformation brought about by the New Covenant effects the healing of man and the deification of the whole person, while it serves as a glorious hymn of praise offered to the Father of lights. Once again, it is in the liturgical action of the Church that we can experience the power of the Resurrection in all its fullness.

This inevitable reference to the liturgy can make us aware of an aspect of the Resurrection mystery that is too often forgotten today. Precisely because the Lord has passed beyond death and patiently leads us along with Himself each day, His relationship with us who are still in death, operates in a "sacramental" way. The sacraments are the instruments of the Holy Spirit, who fashions the children of God in the image of Christ, the Firstborn from the dead. The energy of the risen Christ is communicated through the signs of the first creation, and makes them radiant with the mystery which they signify, so that this mystery becomes a reality for us. It is in the liturgical mystery of the sacrament that we learn to live our new life in the Spirit, for the Liturgy is something very different from a didactic teaching or a simple memorial. It means participation in the life of the living humanity of the Lord, a humanity now hidden in the life of the Father but that nonetheless radiates life into this world.

Finally, this is why our last experience of death, the one that will lead us to the grave, will mean the ultimate authentication of what we already live in the risen Lord. This final participation in the death of Christ will seal the Covenant, already experienced through the many conversions of our earthly life which began with the essential conversion of our baptism.

It is not possible in a few words to go into detail about this progressive illumination that the baptismal energy of the Holy Spirit brings about at all levels of our personality and at all stages of our human growth. In bringing our discussion to a close, however, I would like to underline certain unchanging aspects of this energy which acts from within rather than alongside our psychic life. First of all, the life of the Resurrection is not simply added on to our first, natural life that we inherit from our human family. This points to another aspect: one true being, just as in the case of Christ, is of both man and of God. Christ, the Son of God, was born of the Virgin Mary by the Holy Spirit; not by blood, nor by the will of the flesh, nor by the will of man (John 1:13), but by God, even in his very humanity. In the same way, we are both of man and of God according to the double reading of John 1:12-13. We have been clothed in the image of the earthly Adam, but we are now being clothed in the image of the heavenly Adam (cf. I Cor 15:49). We have been reborn by the Spirit. Our resurrection is "virginal," as was the incarnation of the Word. I greatly fear that behind present day scepticism concerning the virgin birth of Jesus, there lurk two very serious problems: first a basic refusal to accept the mystery of the Resurrection; and second, a resurgence of the old pagan mentality dominated by the dichotomy we spoke of at the outset, a dichotomy that refuses the scandal of a God who is truly man and of a man who is truly deified. The Resurrection concerns above all the divine meaning and destiny of human life.

To forget that our perfected humanity is born from God, like the humanity of the Word who became the firstborn of the new creation, is to tragically misunderstand both the meaning of our sin and the meaning of our redemption. Yet unfortunately this is precisely what is happening in certain currents of naturalistic thinking. Man cannot be healed in depth by psychotherapy any more than death, in all its forms, can be exorcized by science. There is only one Savior of mankind: the dead and resurrected Christ. Perhaps right here is the most urgent and most neglected aspect of the Resurrection for our time. Our century is allergic to ascetical practice. Certainly many elements which are really alien to the Christian mystery have tarnished the purity of the Gospel, elements that run all the way from dualistic

pessimism to naturalistic Pelagianism. But the glorious
Cross, scandal and folly that it may be, remains the
only path that leads towards life.

People in our times refuse—and quite rightly so—to
consider the Cross as a categorical imperative or as an
external constraint. For it is neither of these. The Cross
stands at the very heart of the mystery of life, and this
is why it is Wisdom: How can we escape from the
darkness we find ourselves in without a battle? How
can egotism, injustice, hardness of heart, falsehood,
divisions, human degradation, etc., be removed from
the heart of man without a struggle? This battle that
Christ carried out alone, but for all of us, upon the
Cross must be our own battle as well. We struggle "in
Him" to be sure but such a struggle with our participation is necessary. Otherwise we would merely be saved
from the outside, as it were, like objects, and therefore
we would not be saved at all. Here again, it is the
spiritual realism of the Liturgy which alone can make
us understand that the illuminating power of the Cross
is that of the living God and not that of our own will-
fulness. Only the Cross of Christ reveals itself to be the
power of God; thus the Cross becomes our Resurrection
within our day to day struggle.

I would like to close by mentioning another aspect
of the Holy Spirit's energy that makes me think of the
slogan so widespread today in families and in educa-
tional circles: no complexes and no frustrations! This
concern to avoid "psychological problems" (a concern
not very well thought out) comes from the desire to
avoid injuring people. In reality, however, it represents
a fundamental misunderstanding of man! There is no
need to have white hair to proble the depths of the

death that lurks in the human heart. How, then, can we rid ourselves of death? By feeding its chaos, by maintaining its lie, or by constraining it through social order or moral prohibitions? None of these paths can save man. But Christian ascetical practice is precisely not frustration; it is not some coercion tolerated by Freud and rejected by Marcuse. To the contrary, it is *liberation*. The Cross of Christ that sounds the depths of our life liberates, in the literal sense of setting free, all the lifeforce within us that our sinfulness has held prisoner. The Gospel tells us that this freedom is bought at the price of self-denial, that is, by saying "no" to death and "yes" to Him who is Life itself. Christian ascetical practice is paschal, mystical, theological and lifegiving. It is only by the Cross of Christ that we become free every day, for only the Cross means reconciliation, service, total self-giving, *agapê*.

I think it is superfluous to insist on this point. Just what is the meaning of the Resurrection for our personal lives? At every moment we can verify its meaning—its wisdom and power—by integrating or "recapitulating" in the Resurrection every dimension of the human person. In our final chapter we shall see what this means for our life in society.

CHAPTER 4

The Resurrection and Modern Society

To inquire about the relation between the Mystery
of the Resurrection and the socio-political problems of
our times is certainly not a frequent topic of conversa-
tion these days. But before we begin the search for an
answer to this question, let us first be sure to avoid any
misconception concerning the question itself. If we
understand this inquiry to be a quest for a socio-political
ethic of the Resurrection, I am afraid we'll run into a
dead end, unless we are very clear that what is of primary importance is not an ethic as such, but rather a
"mystique," understood in the specifically Christian
sense of Mystery. If, however, we are trying to discover
a socio-political "technique" or practical application
of the Resurrection, then let us make it clear right
away that we are in a state of total confusion. If we can
rid ourselves of this confusion, however, we should be
able to move ahead towards an answer to this question.

Depending on the circumstances in which each of
us lives out his social and poltical responsibilities, we
can ask ourselves what the Lord's Resurrection means
for the transformation of the economic and political
structures that we may be striving for. Since for us the

risen Christ is a reality of first importance and the very soul of our lives, does it necessarily follow that we have to put forth and strive towards an entire program of action specifically inspired by the Mystery of the Resurrection? On the level of means and methods, certainly not: for that would imply that the Resurrection of Christ is of the same order as the resuscitation of Lazarus, a simple re-animation. But this is not at all its meaning. Christ healed, but He is not "super-thaumaturge." He multiplied loaves of bread, but He does not bring a super-technology to the baking industry. During His earthly life, He already manifested the power of His Resurrection; and this is why St John prefers to speak of the Lord's "signs" rather than of His "miracles." This is all the more appropriate in the period following His Resurrection. Christ acts in our world, and His action is truly "temporal." He does not operate in some other world or some other era, but His action is "new"; it properly belongs to the essential Newness of the Kingdom.

Let us therefore put aside any nostalgia for past Christian ages in which economic and political programs were directly deduced from the Gospel. Strictly speaking, the Church has no "social doctrine." Christ did not come to lay the foundations of financial, economic, and governmental structures. Other religions or ideologies have claimed this type of inspiration, but such a pretense has nothing to do with the risen Christ. It is important to be clear about this: the Kingdom of God, inaugurated by the Resurrection at the very heart of our world, is not some new structure that fell from heaven and stands in competition with the structures developed by our various cultures and societies. Regardless of what people may think who have lost the sense of its Mystery, the Church is not a structure of this kind. In the Church there are only *sacramental* structures, insofar as the Church is the sign by which Christ gives life to this world. The resurrected humanity of the Lord is not a structure of this world: we cannot deduce from it any kind of technical program. The living Christ, and the Church as His sacrament, are not another form of "dough" thrown into this world; they are rather the "leaven of immortality" which must transform the dough of the world. For this reason we insisted earlier that our first task is to acquire a "mystical awareness," a dynamic apprehension of the Christian mystery. Otherwise we shall fail to grasp the true power of the Resurrection.

This does not at all mean that we are to be unconcerned with and detached from social and political struggles: That would be the farthest thing from our thought. What then do we mean? Struggle is certainly necessary. But what struggle? Let us say at once: the struggle for mankind. How is mankind threatened today? Now that is very clear. We know very well the many forms of enslavement that hold man prisoner: injustice, lies, oppression, the tyranny of money, the quest for material possessions, disregard of persons, etc. One criterion allows us constantly to discern the authentic meaning of man: Christ raised from the dead, who is man truly liberated and deified. Christ is not only the light of our discernment but also the strength of our commitment.

This level of awareness, which is genuinely Christian, has far reaching consequences. It is not enough merely to participate with our brethren, whatever their religion may be, in a critical analysis of the conditions of labor and commercial exchange, for example. Our faith in Christ does not confer on us any diploma in economics or sociology and gives us no competence in these areas. Our Christian vision of such factors, however, must go beyond this kind of analysis. First of all in any analysis of the causes of a given situation, we must discern the real and often unconscious motivations of established injustices; then we need to proceed to solutions. If we do not find in the Gospel any political or economic programs, nevertheless we do find a truly revolutionary requirement that runs counter to all of our personal and collective selfishness. We will never be able to rely on packaged solutions worked out ahead of time; rather, in the critical moment itself "the Spirit of your Father will inspire what you are to say."

The essential thing is this: to be witnesses of the Resurrection, with all of the demands and responsibilities such a witness implies. This means, as recent history has shown, that such a witness might well lead to martyrdom. Our only hope, then, is to keep our eyes ceaselessly focused on Him who is the Lord of history, being careful not to quench His Spirit. The relation of the Resurrection to our socio-political problems is properly determined by the evangelical proclamation that Law has been superceded by Grace. As long as we search in the Gospel for a law adapted to the situations of history, we will always be behind the times, and this will lead inevitably to a certain inferiority complex, which is always a bad thing. But we must never forget that we are no longer under the Law. This is precisely the freedom by which Christ has liberated and resurrected us! With regard to our various socio-political problems, even the most complex ones, this means that we must rely on certain inventiveness or fresh imagination that only the Spirit of Christ can call forth within us. For those who live by the Spirit, no law of any kind can give life. If our aim is to work towards an authentic revolution in the spirit of the Gospel, we will first have to measure the conditions of our commitment as new-born creatures of the Holy Spirit.

It should be clear that I am not preaching by this some kind of illuminism or improvisation. Paul also warns us against a way of thinking that would lead us back to the "flesh" (Gal 5:13). If we are animated by the sole concern to *serve,* we will be vigilant, and capable of discerning that which pleases the Lord and that which liberates mankind, on the level of values as much as on the level of means.

Since the Resurrection of the Lord is the ever-present event by which He enters into unlimited Communion with all mankind, we can conclude that this same mystery should become a concrete reality within the sphere of our social life. The Church, the radiating brilliance of the glory of the resurrected One, has no other meaning in the world than to serve as this living sign of Communion. Here again the practical conclusions are not foreseeable. Nevertheless the power of Communion is within us, and it is our obligation to bring it to concrete expression. On an ethical level, this requires that the socio-political behavior of Christian people be characterized by a willingness and a capacity to overcome hyper-sensitivity and hard feelings, as well as by a constant readiness to reopen and renew dialogue. In this regard, Christians must become ever-flowing reservoirs of hope who, without any illusion or naivete, know how to make prayers in an atmosphere of trust. Such hope alone has the power to destroy Death.

It is always invigorating to plunge ourselves back into true Communion in the midst of our daily struggles. I mean that the upbuilding of fraternal relationships among people, an upbuilding towards which we are all striving, remains constantly threatened by death and division, as we know all too well. The Newness of the Resurrection is the introduction into our social structures of a new principal of community, namely, that of divine Communion. This is no program that can be spread by indoctrination; it is rather Life: Trinitarian Life communicated by the Holy Spirit. Unlike the Resurrection, there is nothing spectacular about this Communion, and yet its power is invincible. "This is the victory that has overcome the world, our faith" (1 John 5:4).

It seems that we must read our Christian struggle in this world in the same way that we read the paschal struggle of Christ in the Gospel of the Passion and the Resurrection. We have already noted the contrast between the detailed description of His Passion and the mysterious reticence of the evangelists concerning His Resurrection. For us, it is exactly the same. The Holy Spirit, who continually writes the Gospel in our ecclesial life, makes us attentive to the dramatic circumstances of the passion of man, disfigured as he is and crushed by death and the Prince of this world. Our participation in this drama, however, cannot be that of the passive witness at Calvary. Nor can we in any way contribute actively to human suffering. Our participation must be like that of John, of the Virgin, of the myrrh-bearing

women, and of the Church itself. We must come not
only to know the meaning of the Lord's voluntary death
as the source of liberation for mankind; we must also—
and especially—come to live, here and now in our very
flesh, the paschal mystery of solidarity and redemption.
The Resurrection illumines from within the drama of
the Passion, not only in the Gospel, but also in our own
contemporary social struggles. It is here that we discover the true "mystical" commitment of the Christian
people.

If we wish to make clear the broad lines of this
"Leaven of Resurrection" that we are called to become
in the present-day Passion of mankind, we can affirm
the following: In relation to human labor, our present
struggle to render work with our brothers more truly
human can only be fruitful if we ourselves enter into
God's work which deifies mankind. Work can only be
humanized if man is divinized, and that depends upon
us and upon our witness.

Regarding the difficult struggle to inject a greater
degree of justice in economic relations—for example,
by stabilizing the price of primary resources, which is
the necessary condition for liberating producing coun-
tries still under the yoke of colonization—our "resurrection ethic" consists in struggling to break enslaving
monopolies. Our "Christian mystique" which must inspire such a struggle takes as its source the fundamental
experience of *sharing* characteristics of life in the
Kingdom of God. We affirmed earlier that the risen
Lord in his very humanity is in unlimited Communion
with all mankind. This lifegiving humanity of Christ
now makes its impact upon the world through ourselves
as members of His Body. The ultimate justification for

our existence as baptized people is to spread abroad this divine Communion among all men, a Communion whose spiritual and radiant center is the Body of the living Christ. As confirmation, we should turn ever again to what the book of Acts says about the first community in Jerusalem that lived in the splendor of this marvellous gift of Communion.

With regard to the various networks of social relations, from the family to the labor union and from the cultural circle to the political action group, this same "Christian mystique" will necessarily involve us in a permanent dialectic. For there is a dialectic of community that originates in the Resurrection itself. This dialectic consists in the fact that the specific aspect of mutual understanding between men and nations that derives from God Himself is ceaselessly threatened by the destructive action of the Prince of death. Each one of us has enough experience in trying to live in harmony on the family or professional level to understand what this means. All the poets have sung this drama of love and death, but what we are talking about goes infinitely beyond the simple emotional realtionship between a man and a woman. The dialectic we are speaking of concerns all human relations. The power of the Resurrection acting within us uncovers the lie inherent in the tower of Babel, and its Newness lies in the coming of the Spirit at Pentecost. To remain locked in division would be to submerge ourselves in the dough and no longer be the essential leaven. The power of the resurrected Lord leads us into a new age, marked by the entrance of the Spirit of communion into the arena of human divisions.

It is this same dialectic of Resurrection that in the

past has always made genuine Christians into trouble-some citizens under whatever government they found themselves. For in the "Christian mystique" as applied to political life there is a fundamental rejection, not of authority itself, but of the totalitarian and pseudo-prophetic claims made by every political power. It is enough to reread the book of Revelation if our spiritual vigor in this regard begins to slacken . . .

Finally, we can say that the Christian Newness of the Resurrection, as it concerns our present-day strug-gles, must unceasingly "demythologize" the false proph-ets who lead so many people astray by political power, and at the same time "liturgize" the paschal struggle of humanity that more and more knows bondage yet does not yet know its only Savior. Our Christian condition, therefore, is characterized by an agonizing struggle, we choose neither God against man nor man against God; but like the Suffering Servant and conformed to Him, we choose both God and man in the same love and by the same service. Therein lies our own Cross; and therein lies the hidden Resurrection of all our human brothers. "For while we live we are ceaselessly put to death for Jesus' sake, so that the life of Jesus may be manifested in our mortal flesh. Thus death is at work vigor in this regard begins to slacken . . .